THE BIG SALAD

Written by:
LJ and BK Smith
Illustrations by: Graphic_Tones

Meet Principal Dumble

BK is the co-author of the Baker Series. He is a father of 3 and husband of over 25 years to his wife LJ. He loves all sports. His favorite teams are the Bills, the Sabres, the Rays and the Lakeland Dreadnaughts. He loves children and is very active in the community of Lakeland.

"Good morning students. This is Principal Dumble. I am pleased to announce the annual school play. Each class will present healthy eating ideas. Good luck everyone and have fun!"

Ms. Roll and the class hear the announcement. Allie and Frieda are excited about the school play.

Baker, Tony, Bobbie, and Chris seem worried about being on stage in the school auditorium in front of a crowd of people.

Allie smiles and says, "I love salads. My family always eats them at home."

Frieda replies, "I do too, they taste great."

Ms. Roll says, "That sounds like an excellent idea. We will all select a salad item and present them at the school play."

Ms. Roll asks the students to choose one salad item. Baker and Bobbie are not happy about being in the play because they are shy.

Tony and Chris say that they like snacks better and do not like salads. The four boys all seem unhappy with the choice.

Ms. Roll tells the students that they will pick names of vegetables from a fishbowl. Each student will present their salad item on stage. She tells them to learn a fun fact about their ingredient.

Ms. Roll also announces a surprise field trip to the local farm. Hooray... field trip!

The next day the yellow school bus transports the students and Ms. Roll to the local farm.

Baker, Ally, Bobbie, Frieda, Tony, and Chris are excited to see the animals and beautiful farmland.

Ms. Roll tells the students to pick a basket of their chosen vegetable.

Baker is amazed how round the green heads of lettuce are.

Ally gets her hands dirty pulling the orange carrots out of the ground.

Frieda is surprised how beautiful the stalks of green broccoli look as she puts them in her basket.

Chris fills his basket with huge green cucumbers.

Bobbie uses his muscles to grab the stalks of green celery.

Tony pulls the ripe red tomatoes from their vines.

The students are smiling and having fun as they fill their baskets up and get ready to head back to school.

Enjoying The Big Salad?

Purchase our first book Top of the Muffin, TO YOU!

The next day is the school play. The class and Ms. Roll have worked all week on their costumes and lines. All students, parents, and family members have been invited to the assembly. Principal Dumble welcomes the guests. He announces that Ms. Roll's class will present healthy eating with a variety of salad items.

First up is Baker. He is a big green head of lettuce. Baker was amazed to learn that lettuce is a main ingredient in one of his favorite foods, sub sandwiches. He also learned that lettuce is grown from seeds. Baker was very surprised to learn that lettuce is important for healthy skin, bones, and eyes.

Allie comes on stage next. She is a bright orange carrot. Carrots are the main ingredient in her favorite cake, carrot cake. Allie discovered that carrots are grown underground. She also learned that carrots are important for good vision and a healthy heart.

In dances Tony with a big smile on his face. He is a huge red tomato. Tony is very happy because he learned that his favorite food, pizza, is made with tomatoes to make the sauce. At the farm, Tony picked only the red ones from the vine. He also learned that eating tomatoes helps him from getting sick.

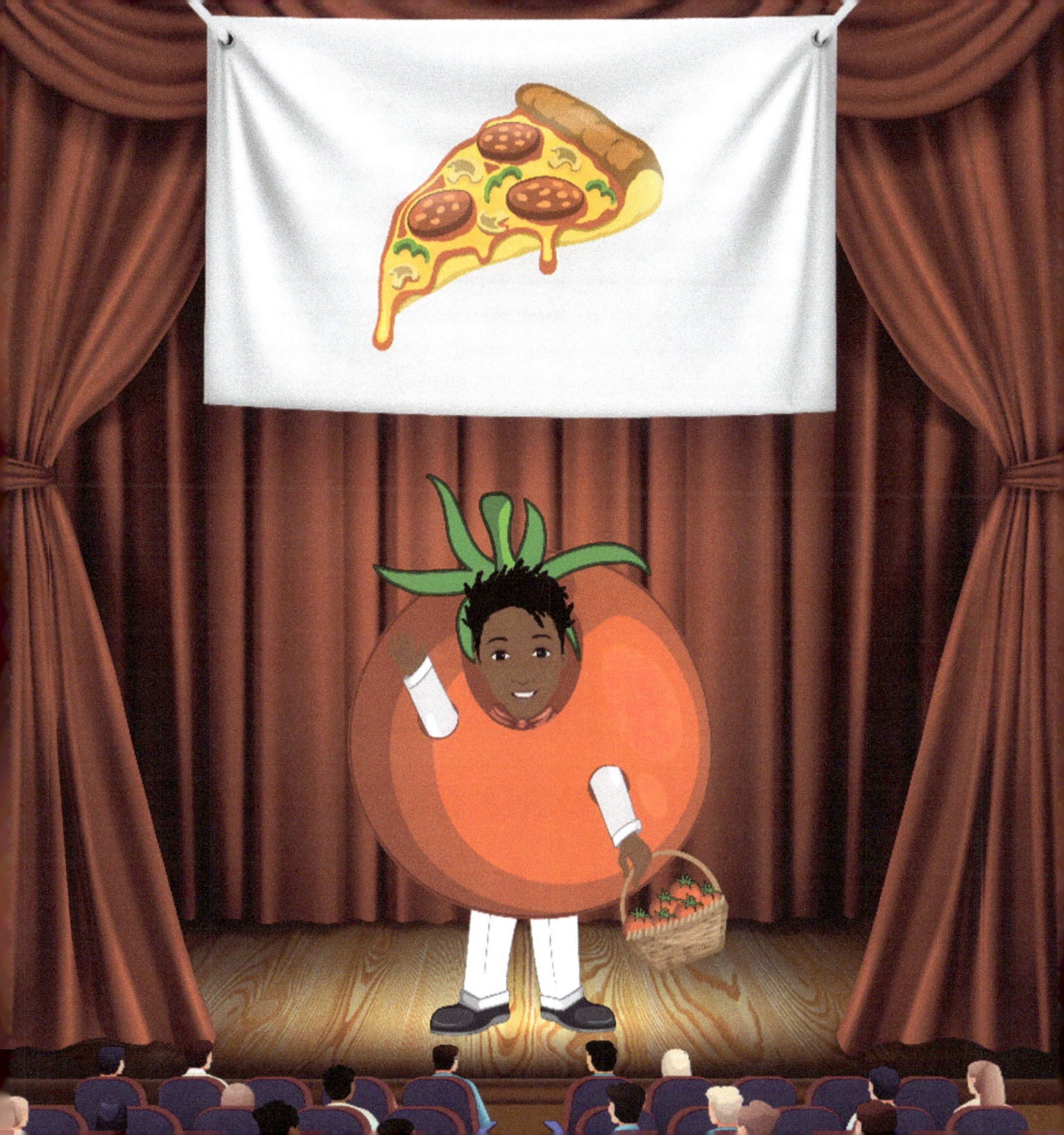

Frieda enters the stage next. She is a stalk of green broccoli. Frieda was blown away by how pretty the flowerettes looked. On the field trip to the farm, she discovered broccoli grows in bundles. Frieda also learned that broccoli helps her hair grow and look beautiful.

Chris is so excited he runs on stage ready to hit a home run. He is a tall cool cucumber. At the farm, Chris picked his cucumbers from a vine. He learned that eating cucumbers helps with adding water to his body hydration, so he can play sports better.

Finally, Bobbie and Ms. Roll come on stage together. Bobbie is a strong stalk of celery. Ms. Roll is the salad dressing that makes all the vegetables work great together. They learned that the celery stalks grow above the ground with leaves on top and roots under the ground. Amazingly, celery has many great health benefits and helps our tummies digest food.

Principal Dumble comes back on stage. He says he is very proud of Ms. Roll's class presentation for healthy eating choices. He thanked the diverse group of students for working together and having fun while learning. Principal Dumble announces, "Ladies and gentlemen, thank you for attending, and I would like to present to you one more time, THE BIG SALAD!"

The class all comes back on stage together for their encore. They are all holding the vegetables they picked at the farm field trip. Each one of them is smiling and happy to have worked together as a team and had so much fun doing the play. As they wave and slide into the big salad bowl, Baker shouts to the audience, "Salad for Everyone!"

Epilogue

And so our journey continues. In our first book "Top of the Muffin to You", our angels learned to make new friends even though they were shy and afraid. Then, in this episode, the group of friends found out that eating healthy foods can be fun. Join our group of special friends for the next adventure in our next chapter coming soon. Summer break is coming and we are cooking up more good times. Join our fan club online and come celebrate with us for fun, puzzles, and games everyday on Facebook page.

We'll see you soon!

Thank you for your purchase!

Leave us a review on our Facebook Page

THE BIG SALAD
Copyright © 2024 By LJ and BK Smith

www.ingramcontent.com/pod-product-compliance
Lightning Source LLC
LaVergne TN
LVHW070535070526
838199LV00075B/6783